ISBN: 978-1-7324413-3-0

Background Information

The art of Flower Cloth or Paj Ntaub is a traditional form of Hmong textile that combines embroidery and reverse appliqué techniques. The geometric patterns hold symbolic meanings in the Hmong culture.

As a young girl at the refugee camp in Thailand, I was taught these techniques and used them to make colorful flower cloths or paj ntaub as a way to support my family. The colorful thread reminded me that better days were ahead.

It is my hope that both children and adults will enjoy this unique art. Each page in this book is filled with different patterns and designs that will open curious minds to a world of creativity and endless possibilities!

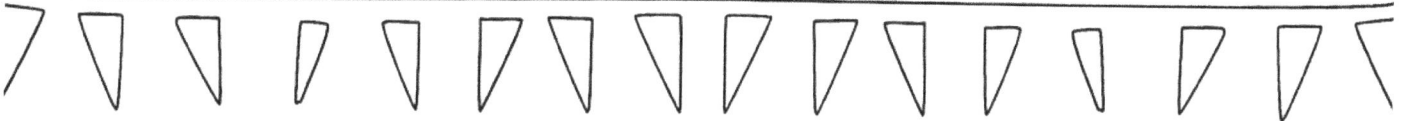

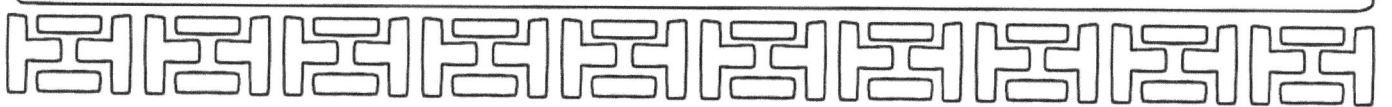